WORLD *of* WONDER

MOUNTAINS

Charlotte Guillain
Chris Madden

words & pictures

For John - CG

To my father-in-law, Paul who
spent his life admiring the view and
rests atop his favorite mountain - CM

Quarto Knows

Quarto is the authority on a wide range of topics.

Quarto educates, entertains and enriches the lives of our readers—enthusiasts and lovers of hands-on living.

www.quartoknows.com

Consultant: Michael Bright
Designer: Victoria Kimonidou
Editor: Harriet Stone
Editorial Director: Laura Knowles
Creative Director: Malena Stojic
Publisher: Maxime Boucknooghe

This edition first published in 2020 by words & pictures,
an imprint of The Quarto Group.
26391 Crown Valley Parkway, Suite 220
Mission Viejo, CA 92691, USA
T: +1 949 380 7510
F: +1 949 380 7575
www.QuartoKnows.com

A CIP record for this book is available from the Library of Congress.

ISBN 978 0 7112 4354 5

Manufactured in Guangdong, China TT012020

9 8 7 6 5 4 3 2 1

FSC www.fsc.org MIX Paper from responsible sources FSC® C016973

Contents

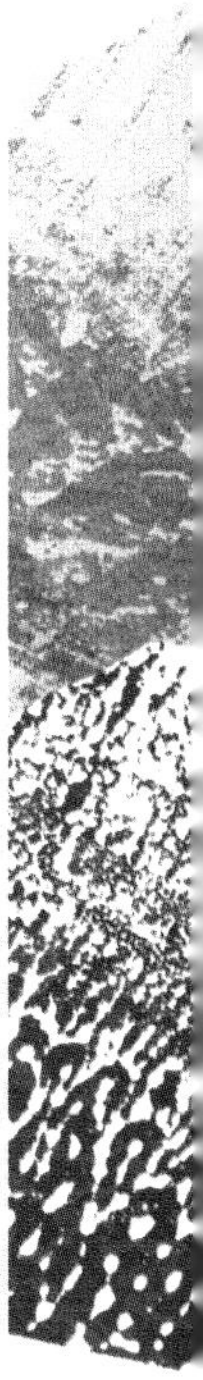

Making a Mountain

Deep beneath our feet, the ground is very slowly shifting. Vast plates of rock pull apart and crash back together. The plates move because they are floating on the Earth's mantle, a layer of soft molten rock.

Long ago, over millions of years, these colossal plates pushed against each other. Rock at the bottom of the oceans crumpled and folded. The rock was forced up and up, until the peaks of mountain ranges appeared above the water.

Slowly and steadily, these towering crags continued to rise as the Earth's plates clashed and pushed the rock ever upward. Today, these fold mountains point toward the sky all over the world, wherever the plates of the Earth's crust meet and collide.

Mountains are continually growing and are constantly being worn away. They are home to unique plants and animals. While some soaring peaks are encased in snow and ice, others explode in a shower of red-hot, volcanic sparks. In a world of wonders, mountains rise above everything else.

The Sky-high Himalayas

A wild wind whips through the high Himalayas, the rooftop of the world. The name means "abode of the snow," as these icy peaks are a world of white. The Himalayas are the highest mountains on the planet.

This majestic mountain range rises high above Asia. Its jagged ridges and crags began forming around 50 million years ago, when the plate of rock beneath India collided with the plate below the rest of Asia. Even now, the Himalayas are still being pushed upward toward the sky. In the far west of the range, the mountain Nanga Parbat is rising faster than any other on the planet. It grows ¼ inch (7 mm) a year.

Glaciers, immense rivers of ice, inch their way down from the steepest heights. There are more glaciers here than anywhere else on Earth, apart from in the polar regions. Lower down, fast-flowing rivers carve their way through the valleys.

As clouds gather to the south of the mountains, heavy rains fall. Rain clouds struggle to travel past the towering summits to the north side of the Himalayas, so the land beyond the mountains is dusty and dry. High up the slopes, the temperature drops. Blizzards rage, ice cracks. Can anything survive in this harsh, frozen landscape?

Peak of Heaven

One towering pyramid stands higher than all the others in the Himalayan range: Mount Everest. This snow-covered giant is the highest mountain on Earth. Its Tibetan name, Chomolungma, means "Goddess Mother of the World." In Nepal, it is known as Sagarmatha, which means "Peak of Heaven." Everest reaches 29,029 feet (8,848 m) up into the clouds, its jagged ridges and sharp peaks dwarfing all below. The slopes of the summit are buried in snow all year round. This snow is deepest at the end of the summer, but the powerful winter winds that whistle across the mountainside blow much of the snow away by spring. It is so cold and bleak at the very top that no animals or plants can survive here.

Spider Survival

One minuscule creature can be found sheltering under a rock, away from the battering wind near the top of Mount Everest. The Himalayan jumping spider is one of the highest living animals on the planet. But how can it survive in this desolate landscape?

As the clouds clear and a beam of sunlight warms the rock, the tiny spider scurries out of the shadows. Its dark-brown body is the perfect camouflage so it can't be seen by birds flapping overhead. The spider is also well hidden from its own prey.

But what does the spider eat, high up where there is so little life? In this bleak habitat, tiny flies and springtails survive on food blown up by the wind. These bugs are the spider's prey. The spider waits until the hairs on its body and legs detect something moving. Its prey is close by.

The spider uses its smaller eyes to spot its prey and then zooms in with its larger eyes. It gets ready to jump by sending more blood flowing to its back legs. Then it fixes a line of silk to the rock before preparing to make its move. When the insect is close enough, the spider jumps…

Deadly Icefall

Sunlight glistens on a shimmering slope that is rough with rugged ice. This is the Khumbu Icefall. It is a steep and creaking section of glacier that is slipping slowly down the slope of Mount Everest.

The icefall moves more quickly than the rest of the glacier, shifting and groaning as gravity pulls it down the sheer face of the mountain.

Huge, teetering towers of ice, called seracs, build up and up as the icefall shudders its way downward. All at once, the glacier judders suddenly and a tower topples, crashing down the slopes in an avalanche of ice.

Fractured Ice

As the icefall creaks and groans again, a jagged crack appears in the brittle surface ice. It quickly grows. The ice splits apart and a crevasse slashes its way through the glacier.

This deadly chasm has sheer, vertical walls that plummet deep down to the base of the icefall. The ice inside glows with a beautiful blue sheen.

Time passes and the glacier moves on. The crevasse starts to close. The rift in the ice has gone. Now nothing but the rough white surface remains, moving relentlessly down the mountainside.

Quiet Queen of the Ice

A stealthy shadow slinks across the snow. Crouching completely still among the rocks, she is almost invisible. A snow leopard is hunting high on the mountainside. Her spot-spattered, gray-white coat hides her as she prowls across the rocky landscape. The wind howls fiercely but her soft, thick fur keeps out the chill. Huge paws stop the snow leopard from sinking into the snow as she makes her silent way across the slopes. Now she leaps from crag to crag, using her long tail to balance. She pauses to take a rest, sheltered from the relentless wind, as she scans the rocky ridge. She is hungry. Her eyes and ears are alert for prey.
She freezes—a wild sheep has begun to pick its way through the rocks toward her, looking for scrubby grass to nibble.
She lies in wait, ready to pounce.

The Nectar Seekers

Lower down the slopes of the Himalayas, grassy meadows grow. In the warm summer months, a carpet of flowers and the hum of insects bring color and life to these grasslands.

Butterflies flit from bloom to bloom. The delicate Blue Apollo butterfly lays eggs in autumn but they don't hatch until the following spring. The plants it eats as a caterpillar make the butterfly taste horrible, and the brightly colored spots on its wings look like eyes, so predators stay away.

A yellow swallowtail flits over plants to feed on sweet nectar. The pointed tails at the bottom of its wings give this butterfly its name.

Deep black and bright blue wings flutter by. It's a blue pansy butterfly. The iridescent insect pauses on the grass and opens its wings to bask in the warm summer sunlight. This butterfly has its own territory and will chase others away.

This common brimstone butterfly spent the winter hibernating in the forests lower down the slopes. Its leaf-like wings kept it hidden in the woodlands, protecting it from predators. Now the summer is here, the common brimstone has flown up the mountain to the meadows, in search of sweet nectar.

Born from Fire

Lying between the Arctic and Atlantic Oceans, Iceland looms out of the cold sea. Over millions of years, two plates of rock deep beneath the island have been slowly pushed apart. Melted rock called magma twists and churns below the surface. The pressure grows. Then, as the huge plates shift and crunch, a crack appears. The red-hot magma whooshes to the surface in a blast of lava and ash.

Iceland's volcanoes have grown gradually, layer by layer. Bands of hardened lava and ash have built up over repeated eruptions. When a volcano erupts, the lava that flows out can also create new mountains.

There are 30 active volcano systems on Iceland, along with others that haven't erupted for more than 10,000 years. Pyramid-shaped Hvannadalshnúkur (pronounced kvan-a-tal-schnu-kir) is the highest mountain on the island. It's the tallest peak of the many that surround a huge volcanic crater.

Ice and Fire

The black winter sky over Iceland is lit up by the flickering, shimmering colors of the Northern Lights. Then a burst of red sparks showers the summit of a mighty volcano rising up over the island. A fiery river glows and flows down the slopes of Eyjafjallajökull (pronounced ay-yah-fyah-lah-yer-kuh-tl). This volcano was dormant for many years, still and sleeping. But now it is active again. Earthquakes move the landscape here and eruptions shake the ground.

Eyjafjallajökull is covered in glaciers. When the volcano erupts, the ice of the glaciers quickly melts and flows down into the valley below. The peak's ice cap makes its eruptions extra explosive. When the red-hot magma rises, the ice melts and water flows into the volcano's crater, where it turns to steam. The steam builds up until...boom! An enormous blast throws clouds of volcanic ash high up into the sky.

The Majestic Alps

The amazing Alps make up the highest and largest mountain range in Europe. Around 65 million years ago, the plate of rock beneath Africa began to smash into the plate under Europe. The rock that makes up the Alps started to push slowly upward. Now the mountains' rocky peaks stretch from France to Slovenia.

Mont Blanc is the highest mountain in the Alps. Its name means 'White Mountain' as the soaring summit is always covered in thick ice and snow.

The four-sided pyramid of the Matterhorn also rises high above its neighboring peaks. It was shaped by the glaciers that slowly slid down from its summit.

Warm air moving from southern Europe hits the Alps. The air rises, clouds grow, and snow and rain fall. The valleys are usually warmer and drier than the higher slopes, but on a crisp winter's day the tops of the mountains can be sunnier and milder than the fog-chilled valleys below.

A Soaring Killer

A golden eagle soars above the rocky ridges of the Matterhorn. Holding his long, brown wings wide, he glides on the warm air rising from the valley below. He doesn't make a sound as he drifts on the breeze, his eyes scouring the slopes below for prey.

The golden-brown feathers on his head and neck give the eagle his name. His dark beak is hooked and powerful, ready to rip and tear his prey.

When he spots a creature moving below, this graceful bird will burst into action with a swift swoop and dive. His sharp, curved talons are the perfect tools for grabbing his kill. Then he will flap and float his way soundlessly back to his mate, to feed in their nest on the high crags.

Deadly Snowslide

A blizzard has been blasting the Alps for days. Wind-blown snow has piled up high on the icy slopes. The storm rages on and the layer of new snow becomes too heavy. It breaks loose from the packed snow beneath it and a deep and deadly rumble is heard in the valley below. Avalanche! Now a frothy cloud billows up into the sky as the massive, sliding snow-pile hurtles down the mountainside. A wall of white fills the air. The avalanche gains speed and more snow is pulled into the thunderous roar as it rushes on and on. The flood of snow buries everything in its path. Finally, the snow-slide slows and the rumble dies away. The valley is silent again.

The Miraculous Mountaineer

A sheer rock face rises up toward the clouds. Birds dive and soar past the craggy cliff. There is no other sign of life. But then something starts to make its way up the dizzyingly steep slope. It's an Alpine ibex, a miraculous mountaineer with impressive curved, ridged horns.

This wild goat's strong, split hooves have sharp edges and curved undersides to grip onto the narrowest sliver of a ledge. Long, strong legs help this gravity-defying climber clamber up the vertical terrain, far away from predators.

With his large lungs, the ibex can take deep breaths as he climbs higher and higher. He fearlessly leaps from rock to rock, grazing on grass, twigs, and moss. Finally, he reaches the clifftop and calmly surveys the scene far below. The intrepid, sky-high ibex.

The Birth of a River

The vast Rhône glacier slowly slides down the slopes of the Swiss Alps. At the bottom of this immense ice-flow, the River Rhône is born. The ice melts and water starts to drip its way downhill. The drips grow into a burble and then into a stream.

The mountainside is rocky and steep here, so the start of the river rushes over rocks, fast and bubbling. The narrow ribbon of water winds and gushes on downward, streaming over rocky rapids and plunging over waterfalls.

Farther down the slope, the river widens and slows. Now the Rhône carves out deep gorges in the valleys below. On and on it glides, slowing at the foot of the mountains and flowing into the largest lake in the Alps, Lake Geneva. From glacier to lake, the river's journey has just begun as it will then flow on toward the sea.

Shy Salamander

Low down on the slopes of the Alps, a gentle rain is falling on the forest. There is no sign of life. But now a tiny, shiny creature emerges and perches on a rock by a babbling brook.

The alpine salamander is normally nocturnal, but the rain has brought it out of its hidden crevice home. Its gleaming black back is grooved and oozes with poison ready to protect it if the salamander senses danger is near.

As the sun sets, the alpine salamander is looking for food. It shoots out its tongue to catch spiders, slugs, worms, and insects. Then, when night draws to an end, the salamander scuttles back into its crack in the rock, hidden once again.

Beetle Music

The sound of chirping fills a meadow in the east of the Alps. The noise is low down in the damp grass. But the chirruping whistle is not a bird. An alpine longhorn beetle is scraping its back leg and part of its wing together. Like a skilled violinist, the endangered insect is making high-pitched music.

This beetle has extra-long striped antennae that curve away from its head, giving the insect its name. Tufts of black hair stick up from the dark stripes on each antenna. Its blotchy blue and black markings help to camouflage it on the bark of the beech trees where it lays its eggs.

Now the beetle stops chirping. It is time to clamber up a flower stem, in search of sweet pollen to eat.

Hawaiian Giant

The island of Hawaii is a jigsaw of volcanoes. A volcanic hotspot lies deep beneath it. When the plate of rock below the Pacific Ocean moves over the hotspot, magma rises to the surface of the ocean, creating new volcanic islands. Hawaii is home to the tallest mountain in the world. While the majestic Mount Everest in the Himalayas is the tallest above the ground, most of the monumental Mauna Kea is under the sea.

Hawaii is known for its warm, tropical climate, but snow and ice lie on the lofty summit of Mauna Kea. It's this snowy cap that gives the volcano its name, which means "White Mountain."

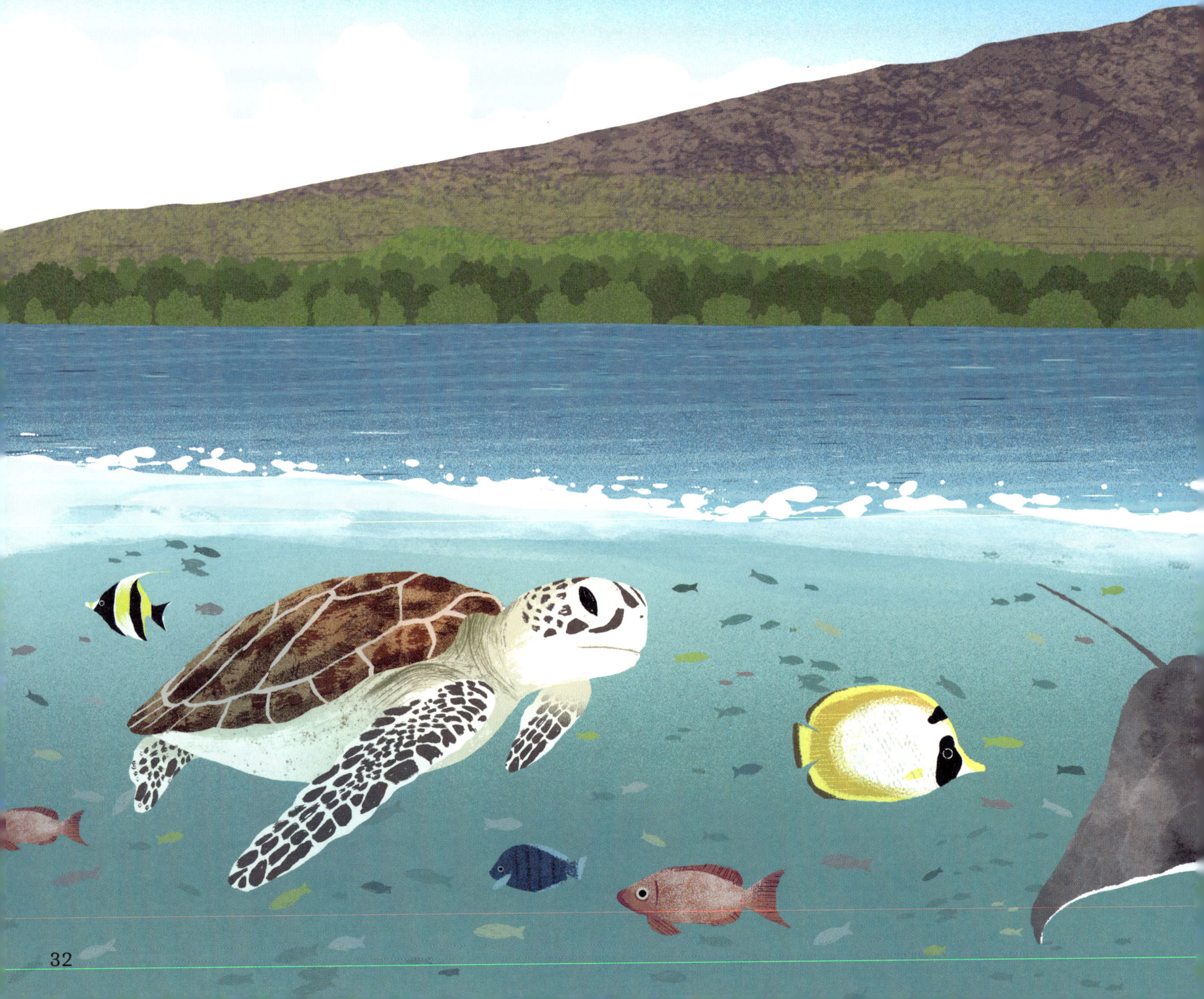

The million-year-old Mauna Kea is a dormant volcano. It hasn't erupted for thousands of years but could spark into life again one day. Mauna Kea is a shield volcano. The lava that erupted from it flowed quickly and smoothly in all directions, giving the mountain shallow sides.

Life thrives both above and below the surface of the ocean around Mauna Kea. Manta rays and green sea turtles swim in the warm waters surrounding the mountain. Above the sea, the endangered Hawaiian hoary bat and the happy-face spider hide in the tropical forest of the lower slopes.

The Ascent of the Andes

The Andes mountains sweep down the western spine of South America, making up the longest mountain range on land. Their name is thought to come from a Native American word meaning "copper." Only the Himalayas rise higher than these towering crags.

Made up of high plateaus and soaring peaks, the Andes mountains began to form around 25 million years ago. The plate of rock beneath South America clashed with a smaller plate under the Pacific Ocean, leading to chains of fold mountains rising upward. There are also many active volcanoes in the Andes. The volcanoes formed when one plate of rock was pushed below another and magma rose to the surface.

The climate can change dramatically from one area of the Andes to another. Tropical rainforests lie just a few miles from icy summits. The north of the mountain range is warm and wet, while in the west of the central Andes the climate is dry and much of the land is desert. In the south the climate is cool and rainy.

Mystery Mountain Dweller

In southern Peru, cool forests nestle in the foothills of the Andes. A lustrous lizard called *Potamites montanicola*, meaning "mountain dweller," makes its hidden home here. This glittering, jewel-scaled creature is something of a mystery.

The *Potamites montanicola* is one of only a few lizards to live so high up, where temperatures are cool. Most reptiles need to warm their blood in the sun before they can become active, but this little lizard seems to be able to get moving without much heat.

The shimmering, colorful reptile is less than an inch long and stays close to pools and streams. Unlike most other lizards, it often takes a swim in the chilly water. During the day, the lizard hides under rocks, saving energy. Then it emerges at night to run across the forest floor in search of food.

A Hidden Hunter

It's dusk. As the sun sets, a cat-shaped silhouette slips among the rocks on the higher slopes of the Andes. Then the tawny-brown, secretive hunter vanishes, expertly blending in with the harsh landscape. This is the mountain lion, also called a cougar or puma. Where has the solitary big cat gone? Two black-backed ears rise up from a rock and turn, listening. A large pair of dark-rimmed, golden eyes scour the slope, searching for movement. The elusive puma stretches and twitches. Has she heard prey coming near? Now she crouches, her strong back legs curled as she waits, ready to pounce off the rock and ambush the unfortunate creature passing below...

A Splash of Pink

High in the Bolivian Andes lies Laguna Colorado—the red lake. Its water is pinkish-red, colored by the algae that grows there. Bright white islands of salt dot the lake, glistening and gleaming under the sunlit, bright blue sky.

Then a surge of pink ripples across the water. Puna flamingos stretch their wings and strut through the salty shallows on spindly, stilt-like legs. These rose-feathered birds gracefully curve their necks down to the lake.

Now, heads upside-down, they filter for food. The water is full of the shrimp and algae they need to survive and which turn their plumage pink. Soon they will stride off again on their pink parade.

High Water

A wide expanse of brilliant blue shimmers in the bright sunlight. The towering, snowcapped peaks of the northern Andes glisten on the horizon. This is one of the highest lakes in the world and the largest lake in South America: Lake Titicaca.

Lake Titicaca lies on a high, dry plateau that stretches between the lofty mountain peaks of the Andes in Peru and Bolivia. Many rivers and streams cascade and meander down from the surrounding mountaintops and empty into the lake, but only one river flows out.

Although the sun beats down on the lake during the day, temperatures plummet at night. The cold weather and the lack of rainfall mean that very little grows around the lake.

Waterbirds wade almost silently through the shallows, dipping their beaks into the water as they feel for food. Meanwhile, beneath the surface, the giant Titicaca water frog scuttles along the cold lake bed. This endangered frog's folded flaps of skin allow it to breathe under water, so it rarely needs to come up for air.

Sunbathing on the Slopes

Toward the highest peaks of the Andes, little life is seen. But when the sun rises on the wind-blown slopes, a small creature slowly creeps out from her underground crevice to soak up some warmth.

The mountain vizcacha is soon surrounded by the other members of her colony, all bathing in the sun's rays to start the day. Eyes almost closed, she curls her long, bushy tail around herself as she lazes in the sunlight.

Soon her soft, thick fur has been warmed. Then the rabbit-like vizcacha hops around the mountainside, searching for moss and grass to eat.

Now her long ears swivel. Her whiskered nose twitches. Another vizcacha calls out in alarm. Has a fox or a big cat climbed so high? The colony scatters, bursting into life as they dart and dash from rock to rock. The vizcacha has vanished.

A Silent Soarer

Higher still, a majestic bird stretches out its wide wings and gracefully glides on the wind over the mountaintops. This is the Andean condor, one of the largest flying birds in the world.

Like shiny black fingertips, feathers fan out from the end of its wings, helping the bird soar and circle silently and effortlessly above the peaks and crags.

The condor's sharp eyes search for animals that have already died on the desolate slopes below. Then, like other vultures, it will swoop down, using its hooked beak to rip its food apart.

A Waiting Volcano

On the island of Honshu in Japan, a cone-shaped volcano towers above the flat landscape. Mount Fuji is the highest mountain in Japan. This striking volcano lies on the join between three plates of rock beneath Earth's surface. Many earthquakes shake Japan when these plates collide.

Mount Fuji hasn't erupted for over 300 years, but it is still an active volcano. It was formed by powerful eruptions that hardened into layers of lava, rock, and ash.

The summit of Mount Fuji is covered in snow for much of the year. Meadows and forests grow on the lower slopes of the mountain. They provide a home for animals, including birds, insects, black bears, and a goat-antelope called the Japanese serow.

For now, Mount Fuji is a beautiful, tranquil place. How long will it be before the volcano erupts again?

The Rugged Rockies

The Rocky Mountains stretch up the west side of North America, from Canada to the southern USA. This fold mountain range began forming millions of years ago, when plates of rock beneath the Pacific Ocean started crashing into the plate below North America. Over thousands of years, huge glaciers also changed the landscape, etching out deep valleys among the crags. Wind and water also wore away the mountainsides, leaving the striking ridges and peaks we see today.

More rain and snow falls in the north of the Rockies, where temperatures fall much lower than in the south.

Forests cover many of the lower slopes, while alpine tundra lies higher up, where no trees can grow. These habitats are home to a wide range of wildlife, from mountain goats and moose to eagles and elk.

Rocky River

A waterlogged meadow lies high in the Rocky Mountains, flooded by a small lake nearby. A stream trickles downhill, away from the meadow. This bubbling brook picks up speed and grows as it flows down the mountainside. It is the start of the mighty Colorado River.

As the water moves on, the river widens and the rock is worn away, creating deep canyons. It rushes over rocky rapids. It surges on through broad valleys and into large lakes. It will then flow on, away from the mountains, across deserts and toward the sea.

Thunderous Falls

A roaring thunder fills the mountain air. Shining spray, like clouds of smoke, billows upward. White water cascades off a cliff edge. This breathtaking waterfall is Lower Yellowstone Falls.

Long ago, a wide river twisted and turned its way over hard, volcanic rock, through the steep-sided valleys of the Rockies. Before long, it reached softer rock. Over time the water wore away the softer rock, leaving a ledge of hard volcanic rhyolite. The river flows over this ledge and rushes downward as a waterfall.

Today, at the foot of the falls is a churning plunge pool, where the torrent of water plummets down. A deep basin has been carved out by the pressure of the falling water. Then the river gushes on, slowly wearing away more of the rock around it.

Mountain Songs

Farther up the slopes of the Rockies, shaded spring sunlight dapples the floor of the spruce forest. The air is filled with the sharp, fresh scent of pine needles. The chirp, chuck, churr of song is all around as tiny birds hop from branch to branch.

Chick-a-dee-dee-dee! A black-bibbed boreal chickadee chirrups and darts about, pecking insects from branches. It hears a twig snap and quickly pops into its nesting hole to hide.

Scuttling silently on the forest floor, a little winter wren forages for food. It bobs and twitches, holding its stumpy tail up in the air as it jabs its pointed beak under logs in search of bugs. It lets out a chatter and trill of high-pitched notes, then creeps away.

Ti-ti-ti! There's a flash of bright orange as a tiny golden-crowned kinglet flits to a higher branch. This male quickly flashes the feathers of his golden crown and gives another high-pitched twitter before disappearing among the pine needles.

Chirrup! Can you hear the whistle of a varied thrush before it fades away? This long-legged, orange-breasted bird uses its beak to pick up fallen leaves as it searches for beetles, ants, and spiders.

A Glacial Lake

The sun is rising behind the jagged heights of the Canadian Rockies. As the sky lightens and shifts from orange to blue, a bright turquoise lake seems to glow.

Surrounded by forests and snowcapped peaks, this is Moraine Lake. It was formed by a huge glacier gouging out the rock and leaving the beautiful lake behind. Piles of boulders from landslides farther up the mountainside are scattered around its shores.

Moraine Lake's deep blue-green sheen comes from the glaciers in the mountains high above. When the ice of these glaciers melts, the water that flows downhill carries fine pieces of rock and soil, called rock flour. The morning sunlight reflects off these particles in the lake water and gives it a beautiful blue hue.

Striped and Stealthy

A slender shape slips through the undergrowth in the woods by a lake. The scaly black back striped with yellow slithers through the scrubby, dry grass. A common garter snake is searching for food.

She has waited for the sun to warm the ground and her scales before starting her hunt. The snake flicks out her forked tongue to smell her prey. Once she has scented her target, she slides soundlessly on, feeling for vibrations and watching closely with her sharp eyes.

The snake may slip into the lake water to pursue her prey of fish, worms, and insects.

When winter comes, the common garter will slink away to her den. There she will hibernate, coiled and tangled around many other sleeping snakes, until spring comes.

Bighorn Battle

On the rocky slopes above the forest, a clashing, cracking sound echoes all around the mountains. Again and again, it repeats with a hard, explosive smash. Smack! Crack!
Two male bighorn sheep are fighting.

The rams rear up on their back legs before crashing their massive curved horns together. These heavy horns are thick and ridged. Their skulls are dense and bony to protect their heads, so they are able to butt and batter for hours at a time. Bash! Smash!

Finally, one bighorn sheep will walk away.
The remaining ram now rules the mountainside.

An Immense Icefield

It is now winter in the Rockies. The frozen landscape is covered in snow. High up among the mountain peaks is an immense icefield, the biggest in the Canadian Rocky Mountains. This is the Columbia Icefield. The vast sheet of ice is a colossal area of connected glaciers. It's all that remains of the deep, dense ice that covered the entire landscape here thousands of years ago. These glaciers are slowly slipping their way down the snowy slopes. Heavy snow has always fallen here in winter, packing and piling up into new ice on the glaciers, replacing the ice that melts into water during summer. What will happen as winters become warmer and less snow falls? How long will the glaciers inch their way down the mountainsides?

Rainbow Rocks

In northwest China, mountains unlike any others rise up in a rainbow of colors. Stripes of orange, gold, blue, and red ripple over the mountainsides. These are the Rainbow Mountains.

The rock of the Rainbow Mountains began to form before the Himalayas rose up above Asia. Millions of years ago, the plate of rock below India crashed into the huge plate of rock beneath China. Layers of compressed sandstone that had been colored by minerals folded upward to form the stripy slopes.

Over thousands of years, wind and rain have worn away the mountainsides, revealing more of the vivid layers of rock. Rusty red sandstone full of iron lies alongside rock stained black by magnetite, yellow by limonite, and green by chlorite.

Smooth cliffs, huge towers, and gaping caves make up the colorful landscape alongside the rippling peaks. This mountain range truly is a wonder of the world.

Protecting our Peaks

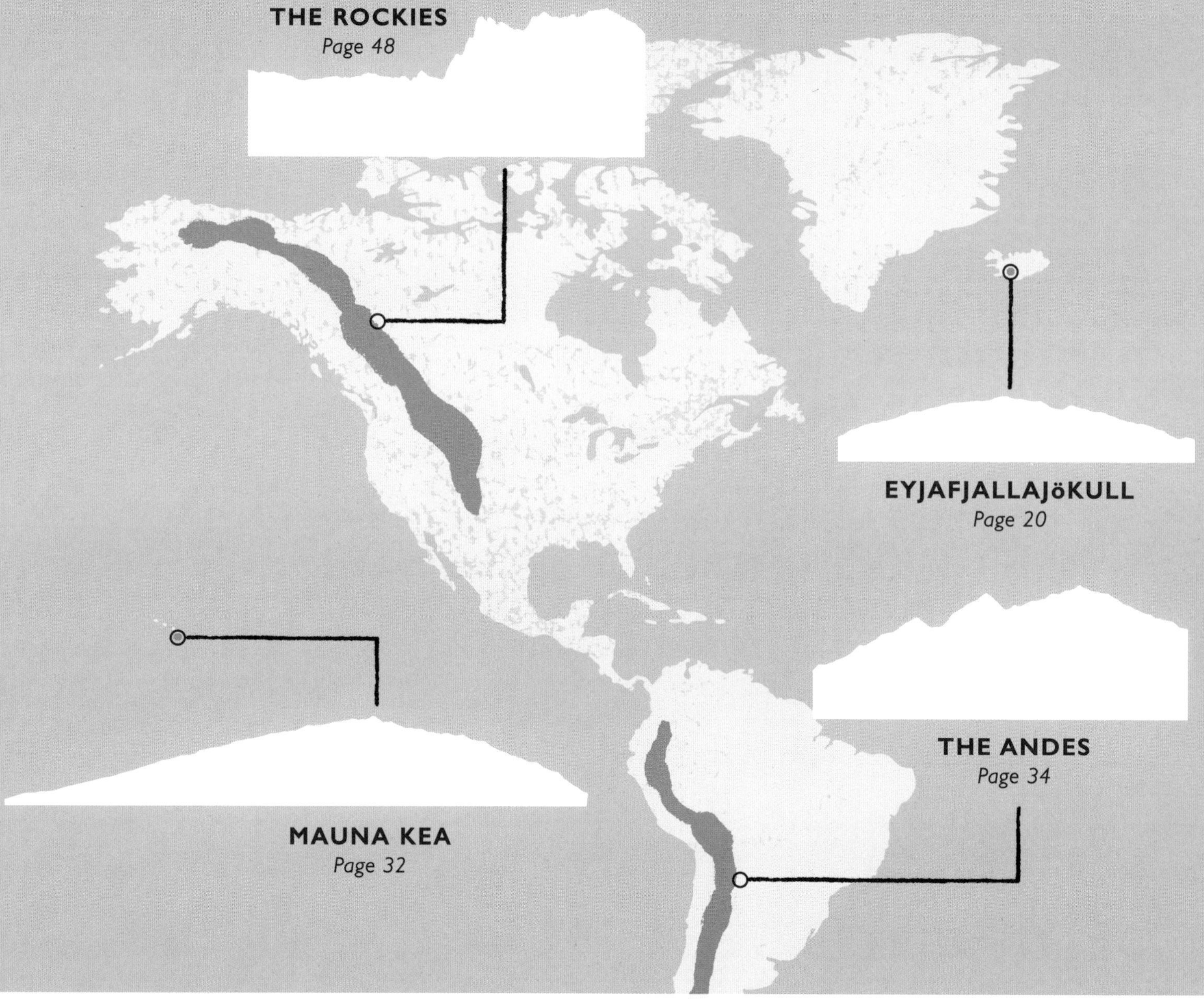

Dear Reader

I grew up in a place without any hills, let alone mountains. I was amazed when I saw my first mountain, in Wales. Since then, I've been lucky enough to ski in the Alps and hike through the Rockies and I would love to explore more of the mountain ranges described in this book. For millions of years, these magnificent mountains have slowly shifted and altered, grown and been worn away. But now mountains are being affected by changes that they have never faced before.

Our climate is getting warmer. Higher temperatures are melting glaciers faster than they can be replaced by winter snowfall. The water from these glaciers keeps billions of people and animals alive. But if the glaciers melt too quickly, the land in the valleys below will flood. Then, when the glaciers are gone, there will be a shortage of fresh water. Without water, wildlife in the valleys, and throughout the world, will disappear.

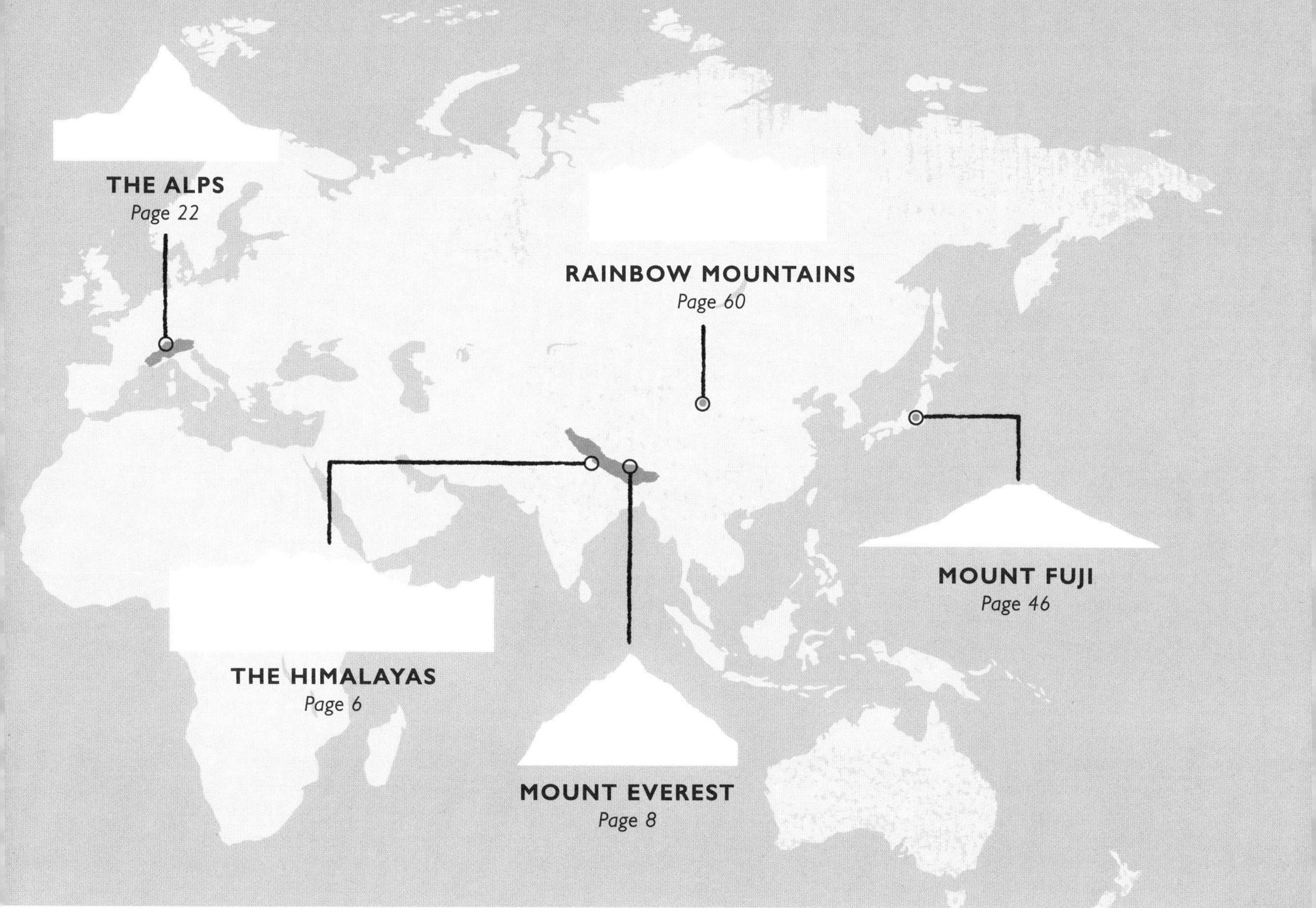

Humans are also cutting down trees on mountainsides, leaving the slopes to be worn away quickly by wind and rain. Many species that live on mountains are endangered, such as the Hawaiian hoary bat, the snow leopard, and the giant Titicaca water frog.

You can support organizations that help to protect mountain habitats so these creatures can survive. Humans must start planting trees on mountainsides and stop cutting them down. We can all help to limit the rise in global temperatures by reducing the amount of energy we use and by using sustainable energy. I hope this book will inspire you to tell your friends about the ways we can work hard to care for our mountains. Together we can help to make sure they are there for millions of years to come.

- Charlotte Guillain

Index

Find Out More

Books

Everest by Sangma Francis and Lisk Feng (Flying Eye Books)
The Snow Leopard by Jackie Morris (Graffeg Books)
Bird's Eye View: The Natural World by John Farndon and Paul Boston (words & pictures)
Geo Detectives: Volcanoes and Earthquakes by Chris Oxlade, Anita Ganeri and Paulina Morgan (QEB)

Websites

Visit the National Geographic website for kids to find out more about volcanoes: www.natgeokids.com
Learn about the wildlife of the Himalayas and the threats that mountains are facing on the WWF website: www.worldwildlife.org
Find out more about the animals of the Rocky Mountains on this National Parks website: www.nps.gov
You can see pictures of glaciers and crevasses around the world on this website: www.nationalgeographic.org